Elixir is a multi-personaed action movie, a love poem, a trip down memory lane, a Kulchur lexicon, an ode to NYC and tribute to exotic ports everywhere. It's a tender balm for the paranoid and lonely, and a tentacular tonic for the heart of Time. I loved, once married, and have kept attentive to half a century and more writing of this genius of The Poem. Lewis Warsh opens the doors of perception with wit, suspense, beauty, surprise.
— Anne Waldman

I want to talk about how beautiful a book *Elixir* is, and describe its mastery, and soulfulness, but then I imagine Lewis teasing me about using "mastery," then teasing the word itself, then placing it in five different phrases to create a tonal scale out of amusement and precision. There are so many layers of possibility Lewis Warsh tended to in his writing, without signaling that he was doing so, which make the poetry inviting and mysterious—steeped in recognition of common experience and wry depths of personal idiosyncrasy. His sense for arrangement of line and sentence across formal vessels that allow everything to be let in and go together is one I've loved and learned from for years. To have this book is to have a gift to dive into.
— Anselm Berrigan

I'll never forget hearing Lewis Warsh read for the first time, how he kept the room in a trance, at the edge of every line, leaning ever forward. The book was called *Inseparable*, its poetry driven by an associational logic that is key to the form his work took on over the last few decades. A collage so seamless maybe it's not, a song drifts in and out the window, changing the view but not the tone, which stays with you as the story keeps shifting stanza by stanza, like life itself. *Elixir* is the latest collection of this dark and playful work, which has changed my sense of what's possible in language. This is poetry that comes back to haunt you in the end. My favorite kind.
— Ryan Eckes

Lewis Warsh's *Elixir* gathers the fragments of memory: song lyrics, novel titles, oft-repeated phrases whose meanings transform with time. His gentle voice comes through the lines, measuring time by touching the lives and afterlives of every character who walks through his poems—students, workers, neighbors, exes, lovers. Open *Elixir* to "look through the keyhole and see who's there."
— Lyric Hunter

Elixir is a stunning final collection of poems by Lewis Warsh, full of jokes, music, melancholic flashes, meanderings, and surprises ("The sunlight on the sand is breathing beneath your skin"). It's also a practical handbook of possible 21st century poetic forms, with a wide range of lyric prowess enhanced by memory and humor, looking back on seven decades of reading, writing & publishing. New York City is the *locus* of the page, a place for and of the poem from start to finish, along with a confluence of personal geographies, glimpses of lives and friends in Cambridge and western Massachusetts in the 1970s and San Francisco and Bolinas in the 1960s ("There are many street corners where last / Conversations took place—"). Reading this book I think of David Bowie's *Blackstar* and George Harrison's *Brainwashed*, where death is acknowledged in the songs, a posthumous masterpiece. A *tour de force* with an absolutely modern sense of poetry as a living craft.
— Guillermo Parra

ELIXIR

ISBN 978-1-946433-93-0
First Edition, First Printing, 2022

Ugly Duckling Presse
The Old American Can Factory
232 Third Street #E-303
Brooklyn, NY 11215
uglyducklingpresse.org

Distributed in the USA by SPD/Small Press Distribution
Distributed in the UK by Inpress Books

Cover artwork: Lewis Warsh, *La Disparition #2*, 2009, collage on board, 15 x 20 inches
Cover design by Max Warsh
Book design and typesetting by Jada Gordon and goodutopian
The type is Bell MT

Printed and bound at G&H Soho
Covers printed offset at Prestige Printing and letterpress at Ugly Duckling Presse

The publication of this book was made possible, in part, by a grant from the National
Endowment for the Arts, by public funds from the New York City Department of Cultural
Affairs in partnership with the City Council, and by the New York State Council on the Arts
with the support of the Office of the Governor and the New York State Legislature. This
project is supported by the Robert Rauschenberg Foundation.

ELIXIR

LEWIS WARSH

UGLY DUCKLING PRESSE
BROOKLYN, NY

for Katt Lissard

for Zola Ray Warsh & Veera May Warsh

CONTENTS

NIGHT SKY

Night-life in the country,
beyond the sighting
of a raccoon,

and the headlights
of a pick-up returning from the
dump

night-life in the treetops. The
3-legged dog next door
doesn't bite. Do I hold

on for a moment or do
I slip over the edge?

Night-time in the
parking lot outside
Arizona Pizza, the Metro

North train
arrives in Wassaic, I get
off at the last stop.

Tuesday matinees
at the Triplex. The forklift
operator's wife at the end
of the bar.

Night-life in the Bronx.
A dead carnation
in your lapel.

My mother knots my tie
before I walk out the door.

Night-life on the Pacific
Rim. I wear a bullet-proof vest
in Coconut Grove.

Night-life anywhere filled
with stars in the night sky.

Night-life in the baggage
claim area with no where
to go.

STOWAWAY PANTHEON

1

I saw you from a distance but
you turned away
as if you didn't know me, and
then I saw you up close

and it was someone else
but you said "hello"
like ships in the night

you were coming up the aisle
and I was going down
to my seat in the front row
and you were calling my name
from the top balcony

and I was sipping a cold one on the edge
of the pier and watching the dancers
on the waves when you walked by
for the first or second time

and I didn't remember your
name under the purple
sky but as you turned to leave

I asked you to stay
or maybe I said "hey!"
and you didn't hear

2

Pots and pans need to be scrubbed
with Brillo.

Sometimes penicillin is needed
to cure the common cold. Free

flu shots are available in the local
drugstore, if you didn't know.

High tide, flash flooding, an old
pickup with a clutch.

Split the difference or rake in
the chips.

A glass of hot milk in the dead
of night.

A slice of pie à la mode (left over
from yesterday)

for the road ahead.

3

The twist has been out of fashion
for decades. All you have to do is stand

in one place and move your hips.
It would seem like you might want

to count your blessings for having
survived this long into a future

you never thought was coming. Better
melt back into the night before

anyone recognizes you, and calls
your name.

4

I'll go on record and say
everything twice, in case no one hears,

and you can play the record back one word
at a time and you might even translate

what I said into a different language so
"I don't know what you're talking

about" might be something she said in

response to something I was thinking

out loud, something I said
to someone else

in another life.

5

It's time to collect our coats
and go home
but there aren't any coats
and there isn't any home.

Do the math, for god's sake,
and make it come out right, tonight,

on the road between
Albany and Troy.

6

It occurs to me that
the world could end
at any moment

but sometimes I think
it could go on forever
as well. The idea

of the world ending
makes more sense
than imagining some

kind of endless future
that might include people
walking around on other

planets and never kissing.
In the scenario about ending
now I see an absence of water,

a cloud in front of the sun,
I see scorched earth
and the bodies of fish floating

on their backs. I see some
tumbleweeds blowing across

the floor of the ocean

and a lot of bones.

7

afterthought
blemishes

stationary
viaduct

hotel room
indents

expectation
inhabit

perseveres
armband

forsaken
kiosk

inanimate
peristalsis

Ovaltine
penumbra

somnambulism
infection

absent
proprietor

scapegoat
dyspeptic

humidifier
sandwiched

mainland
rivulets

retired
ombudsman

zipper
anesthesia

bellicose
microwave

humbug
Mediterranean

vintage
caramel

stowaway
pantheon

OLD FLAME

There are movies that come back
to haunt you at the end
and you can hear the music building
to a crescendo like Hollywood
so you in the audience and you in the
starring role are almost the same
good looking clean cut up tight all of
the above and none
I wouldn't recognize you on a bus
if you paid me
to get on and off
and you wouldn't remember my name
for all the nights in the world
we crawled into bed
with the lights on
and the radio playing
soft and low
we might as well have been blind-
sided by a two-ton truck
for all it matters
because there's only the present
like a movie played backwards
with a cast of thousands
hanging on for dear life.

ALMOST NOTHING

I had some thoughts, embedded
inside other thoughts, which took shape
against a background of cloudless
skies,

and a volcano in the distance
erupted and all the people who lived
in the foothills were buried under
tons of white-hot lava and the butcher

put his thumbs on the scale and the
prices went through the ceiling, the
price of chop meat, for instance, almost
doubled over night, and coffee

beans were parceled out a quarter pound
to a customer in brown paper bags so
you couldn't tell whether you were getting
decaf or regular

and it all smelled the same,
the dust particles in the air, the perfume
of the woman pressed against you in
the Tube, it all tasted the same,

a different version of what had happened
before, the piranhas crawling out of
the bush to lick the dried blood
from the corners of your mouth,

an open door to the past
where you're always welcome, a gypsy

cab ride to the edge of town where
you put out your thumb and hope for the best,

and maybe you'll have to spend another sleepless
night on the shoulder of the broken highway
the coyotes chanting your name like an anthem
from star to star

GRAND HOTEL

for Joanne Kyger

1

Tell someone what
you need and see what
happens. "Nothing,"
I said (instead), "I don't
need anything."

That was last year—even
the syntax is different now.
Pigs with nose-rings.
Haven't we met
before?

Once I was a chauffeur
with jelly for brains.
Now I stand on the tip of an obelisk
with all of Paris
at my feet.

The truth is
to say something
once and then say it again
in a different way
until it means something else.

A circle inside
a square revolves
in air. The deer and
the llama on the banks
of the Loire.

2

Address the question of going,
losing out, staying behind.

The light of the stars ebbs and flows
across the water.

Someone's in a quandary, you can't
remember her name.

Prepare for the future,
and what it might bring.

A whale watch off the Gloucester coast.

An all you can eat buffet ("I'm afraid we're out
of the Crab Louie")

We go on vacation it rains all the time.

Impertinent waves of bliss.
A dog and a bone.

The termites gnaw a hole
in the roof of your house.

You can repeat everything I told you,
but who wants to know?

3

There's no where to go but up
when you're on the bottom, or so they say

The river is deep
but the hole is deeper

There's a big drop on either side
so stay close to the center

You can meet and greet whoever comes your way
with a straight face

You can fall asleep on the living room rug
with a dog at your feet

Fido, that's his name,
he comes when I call

"Fido," I say, in my sleep,
and he comes running, over hill and dale.

4

Let's travel in the realms of gold
paint, more dead than alive.
"I haven't seen you in years."
"You haven't changed an aorta."
"Don't change any part of you."
"I hate the way you are."

Half-hearted attempt to put
arms through sleeves of sweater.
There's no where to go but
below sea level and beyond. Call me
when you reach the bottom.
It takes all my strength just to nod in

your direction. House near ocean,
just a shack in someone's eyes.

They could be anyone or no one.
A neighbor waves from a car. It's
six hours earlier. I'll take you to lunch
at the Hula Grill. Achieve something
without dying. Discover something
beneath the stones. The terminal point
of misunderstanding
begins and ends at your door.
Died in the process of unearthing
whatever.

Armed men on street corner.
"Dejected and silent."
Himmelweg, the road to heaven.
No standbys, no flights.

5

There was a rumor that the leading lady was being poisoned
by her understudy. I call the waitress to bring us our check. The
bone of the whale's thigh caresses the back of my thumb. There's
a dog leashed to a fire hydrant at the end of the alley. Most people
go to bed early, or read in bed until they fall asleep. The sushi bar
has gone out of business. One person enters, sits down, orders a
drink. Then another person comes in, orders another drink, and
they begin talking.

Remember what Robbe-Grillet had to say about the novel?
The measure of it all was that night and day are not the same.
Arbitration might lead to a higher salary, a dead end job in a
one-horse town. You have to choose between your career and your
marriage, but not tonight.

Solitude: move through
the trees. The door to the
trees.

A river. Solitude: windows.
The wind passes through

the tops of the trees.
Solitude: a bridge crossing
a river in the middle

of night. Solitude:
I stand on the edge of
the river.

("It's not a bad life.")

7

The slush fund is empty
and there's no end in sight.

It comes out of the ground

like a kiss, in
slow motion. My

alma mater calls up asking
for a donation. Small bills

please. Fives and ones.
A ranch hand pours a bucket

of ice water
over his head.

Even the perennials
need to be replenished
in the spring. It

takes some time for
the truth to sink in.

A little body warmth
on a cold day

in a room at
the end of nowhere.

8

Someone's mother might be calling you home for dinner,
a long table with a maid and a large spoon for the soup. Now
you can downgrade thinking to a black & white photograph
and a song on the record player, "Hold On, I'm Comin'." You
found it in the attic, hidden in the corners, where everything
gathers dust like everything you ever left behind, until the
closet door opens and we fly like birds of a feather into the great
unknown. Then the record changes and we put our feet up
on the table one last time before going to bed. Somewhere
there's a bed & breakfast just for us, as in the song "Somewhere"
from the cast album of *West Side Story*, don't you know?
I'd like to say, "just call me, and I'll be there," but I can't. It's
hard to make promises you can't keep, as another song goes,
but at this point the narrative breaks off and the audience
heads for the exits. We have a long drive, so wish us safe
voyage. Patches of ice float down the windshield in slow

motion. As soon as I finish my sentence (no, don't interrupt
me) you can leave.

9

There's a void between
the person I used to be and
the person I've become: what
of it?

Chances are the same is true
for you, or someone you know.
The margin of error
is less than zero.

Come as you are or take
the long way home. I can see
the freckles on your neck
in the cold light of day. How

about a sandwich
on a paper plate and
some tonic in a thin-
stemmed glass?

I'll just be a minute.
You can sustain the old
myths for only so long
before the food turns cold

on the roof of your mouth,
and the songs
on the car radio
fade into the night,

"Bye Bye Love," "Wake
Up Little Susie," "All I Have

to Do is Dream," "Devoted
to You."

10

Wade in at neap tide when the water is cold.
The ten most wanted are still at large.

I climb the ladder to the bird's nest
and point my binoculars out to sea,
like Captain Ahab with his wooden leg
on the lookout for Moby D.

It's best to bite your tongue
until the pain goes away. "I haven't seen
that guy since high school," you think

(without speaking).

The word "great" must appear in every sentence.
Concepts like "the word made flesh" must
appear under the sheets.

"Coffee," I shouted, into the abyss,
but no one heard.

My lips were moving but the words
were trapped inside my head and wouldn't
come out, like the words to a song by

Frankie Laine from the 1950s, "The
Old Master Painter," which I sometimes
sing to myself in the shower.

Ask the blonde in the pink blouse
with the poodles for directions.

The light at the end of the tunnel,
wherever that is.

11

You can see it coming, like a shooting
star. Something inevitable was happening,
but you didn't know it. First you had
a dream that it was happening and then you
made it happen—"in real time." It was an
eye opener, to say the least, to know
that was possible. You could even
have a daydream or a fantasy and then it
would suddenly happen. You didn't have
to do anything to make it happen. All
you had to do was be there in real time.

The first time that happened—I'm dreaming
back now, going back. I'm there, I'm almost
there. There's a restaurant, in the Midwest,
that's all I know. Waking up, there's a body,
I can see her face. That's it for today. Thank
you for your time. That time, now, then—I can
go back over it. You can say one thing
and then you can leave. I don't have any
money—can I pay you next week?

I didn't say anything.

ON JOHNSON ROAD

I took a walk down Johnson
Hill Road to see the beaver
build her dam. But she wasn't
there, only a few ripples
on the surface of the pond.
A few flies alighted on my shoulder,
and in my hair. Then I sat
out for awhile and read a book
about Jean-Paul Sartre and
Simone de Beauvoir. I haven't
come to the good part yet,
sex in the grass. Then a few
raindrops fell on my head.
There's the path into the woods
behind the house, lost in shadow.
That's where I'm going, just give
me time. It seems to get late
early, or earlier, each day, which
isn't exactly news to anyone,
but something to say, as each
hour a little more light vanishes
from the sky and the barred owl
sounds its cry from the uppermost
branch, and the leaves begin to
sway, and turn color, overnight.
Soon it will be autumn and all
the fall colors and a few deer will
dare to walk across the road without
fear of hunters or people in fast
cars. Soon the seasons will change;
the grass turn brown, the leaves
purple, like old wine, and the prosecutor

will present inadmissible evidence
to the jury of one's peers, whoever
they might be, old, young, blind,
aging, embittered, dissolute,
and dumb.

LAST JUDGEMENT

You might think The Last Judgement is already at hand

Even if you make your escape, there's no where to go

She interrupted me as soon as I started talking

My credit card is invalid, my arm is in a sling

The landscape rolls by, even when you're sleeping

I wouldn't call if it wasn't an emergency

You can go into the corner and sulk like a baby

Go back to the beginning and repeat everything you said

A patch of snow at the base of a tree, the smell of persimmon

Come to bed before it gets too late and the sun rises for the
    last time

Place the shore in its proper relation to the birds in the sky

You can learn the foxtrot in three easy lessons

Wiped my boots on the welcome mat and sold my soul
    to the company store

Late afternoon muscle tone, a backyard fizzle

A coin falls through a slot and lands in the dust

There used to be a nail salon around here, there used to be
    a car rental agency

I lounge about hawking my credentials through a filter

I'll call you when I'm in town, but I don't know where you are

The curvature of the spine is no longer incurable

I'd take you up on your offer but I'm hard of hearing

Turn up the volume if you want to hear the birds

A suspicious van was discovered on a street near Times Square

Keep your mouth shut and nothing will happen to you and
    your friends

Do I run on ahead of myself or do I bend with every thought?

I take off my socks and put my head under the fire hydrant

All hell breaks loose when you close your eyes

I can take home what you can't eat and feed it to my dog

The door opens and woof-woof—the air disappears

A woman with a toothpick at the company picnic
    catches your eye

Wore out my welcome and disappeared up the chimney,
    like Scrooge

The knives and forks take on a life of their own,
    but all the spoons are bent out of shape

It's possible to disappear into thin air, like a kiss

The conductor shouts "all aboard" but I'm asleep on my feet

A flock of paralegals sing The 1812 Overture before dawn

"Call for back up," one might say, as the clouds pass in front of
    the sun

You might fall asleep in the snow and never awaken

Maybe we met by accident or were introduced by someone we
    knew

The lesser of two evils shows up on my doorstep with a
    warrant

Quiet intervals, synthetic drapes, a reflection in still water

I confuse two people on a bed in my head

I arrive empty-handed: no suitcases, no referendums,
    no slugs

HERE WE ARE

Here we are back on Shattuck Avenue
of all places. Don't say I didn't warn you.
All the ghosts are still alive. Some
strange dude from your distant past
might even step out of the shadows.
Nothing surprises me. You can linger
over a croissant until your hair turns gray,
but then what? The late evening fog is coming
in over the tops of the hills. There's an all night
CVS right around the corner. A thumbnail
sketch of my heart on the bathroom wall.
A ransom note written in invisible ink.
Sometimes adversity works in your favor.
Liquid Plumber might come in handy
if the pipes are clogged. A mail-order bride
steps off a train into the arms of a stranger.
All the dark places where we used to go are
still open for business. Everything is
half-price. You can cross against the light
if you see me coming. Shattuck Ave,
lost in the afterglow.

AU GRATIN

I mistook you for someone I knew
on the B train

It came on time and then it sat
disconsolate
in the station

and everyone stared into the eyes
of the strangers across the aisle,
men and women both

some with 3-fingered gloves
took the time to apply lip gloss
in preparation for the night ahead

the bed, the distribution rights,
the women in grass skirts

a mountain
of red ants, mock turtle soup

under a low flame.

AGENCY OF THE LETTER

Come to me, as one who might
want love of anyone, more or less,
and I'll take care of those who
live their lives in abeyance, held
at arm's length out of fear that
at any moment they might burst into
flames if they equate themselves
with their feelings, or even worse,
go unnoticed by the very people
whose attention they desire. Everything
depends on finding a point of unity,
of transforming yourself into a
contemptible person, the maître d'
who turns people away because
they're improperly dressed. Faithlessness
will cost her her life. As buds grow,
as the forest murmurs, as a page
of ancient letters is pasted
onto a canvas. Even if we wanted
to we couldn't blend in. As different
as the present might seem from
the old days, even a few months
distant, when limited contact
was permissible, when eye-to-eye
contact was frowned upon, when
even a kiss would cost dearly.
So badly did we mistake ourselves
in the colors of the sun. As
far away as the distance between
Venus and the sun. As far as a cloud,
when it blocks out light.

ANYTHING YOU SAY

We live in an occupied zone among despots & thieves

The birds drop in uninvited, nameless blossoms fall to the
ground

One might as well pee on the street & hope a police car
doesn't pass

This is the derivation of *cogitare*, to collect one's thoughts

He put the barrel of the revolver inside his mouth, but
nothing happened

I have to change my seat because the sun is in my eyes

The dead animals were left to rot on the prairie

You can't survive without paying attention to everything

A spontaneous reaction is a true reflection of a person's
nature

She was like a bird—she *was* the bird—wading into the foam

I write the same poem again & again without meaning to

The time of year is more important than the time of day

All we need is a photograph to recapture the past

The impulse to continue (what will happen next?)—the
impulse to end (how will it end?)

It's the first warm day of spring but I'm not leaving the house

Small details—the lemon-yellow curtains—the bubbles on the
   edge of the glass

Sap hardens on the bark of a tree or drips into a pail

He took a photograph of the inside of her heart, but it didn't
   come out

The people on the shore are waving their arms in your direction
   but nothing they do will keep you from going under

The photograph was blurred except for her lips & eyes

Possibly the person listening to you will forget what you said

He put his elbow on the table & rested his chin in his palm

You can say anything, in the moment, with the hope that no one
   will care

The arrow passed through her ribcage & entered her heart

You took the words out of my mouth & threw them out the
   window

My mind is an open system, but the doors are closing

Life is more than a series of broken promises

Pieces of a body fall from the sky to create a new person

You can use the word "sweet" to describe almost anything

The closer we get to someone the farther away it seems

I was looking for something I had lost but it was right in
    front of my eyes

Unassuming yellow fish swim up out of the coral

The phone was ringing off the hook in my head

Interlocking flashbacks, role reversals, the gauge of
    ambivalence

You can be anywhere in your mind & no one will notice

Envy needs an object when the night is still

Her thoughts are like a series of windows covered with dust

The dancer was blinded by the light of a flashbulb & hurt her
    knee

My love came to me vacant-eyed in a kind of delirium

The dog was vomiting on the side of the fire hydrant

A storm warning is in effect for the tri-state area

Apply some hot wax to the wounds on my back

It's easy to promise something you can never give

I drive him to a store where he can buy some long johns

She refuses to be interviewed on camera but she'll talk off the
    record

The 7th-Day Adventist hands me a pamphlet

You can fall asleep in the rain and no one will care

The people who were before us left a stain on the sand

The sunlight on the sand is breathing beneath your skin

SHELTER ISLAND

There was no water or sound,
standing at the window in
the evening. That was the

best moment: walking by the
water's edge in the evening.
Uncovering stones, with mollusks

on them: prepare them for
dinner or throw them back in.
They cling to the underbelly

of a rock at the water's edge.
Guten Abend, I said, but it was
late, it was beyond the

time of day where the sound
of the water weighed on my heart,
as I slept rocking forward

as the light poured over the stones.
It was neither the beginning
nor the end of our life. There's

an outside chance we'll
be at your place by nightfall.
Guten Nacht, I said, unabashed

as I kissed you good night.
For love had already faded
across the sky. It was not that late.

STATE OF GRACE

It's almost impossible
to focus on knowing anything
when later in the day
you've forgotten it already
and it all comes back like a ghost
in your arms only to vanish
as the sun rises in the west

and Xmas comes once a year
and Franz Ferdinand was assassinated
and the total number of casualties were never
added up, not the dogs or the stray cats
who were caught in the crossfire
on a day like this one when you step outside
yourself for a moment and see the
light on the grass, a moment

of intoxication from zero to ten and
then you are off the charts
and wedding bells are ringing but
not for you, and the bride in white
huddles in the backseat of a Chevy
Impala not knowing where
the wind is taking her and whether
or not you take no for an answer
or a question you will never pass
this way again so just remember

to hold on tight and make every moment
count for something in the long trail
of clouds and smoke and pollen and adjust
your gas mask when you walk downtown after

dark and breathe in the undetected particles
from another world

and it's all downhill from here but
you don't want to know, it's all over
except for the shouting, and across the
river you can hear the bugler play "Taps"
to the birds in the trees as the sun goes down
one last time and maybe

alcoholic beverages are served to minors, even
kids under ten line up at the bar for shots, and maybe
it doesn't matter when the mist rises there
are only a few people on board who look familiar
from the last time around and these will be your
friends for life (or so you think) and maybe this is the
start of something new, as the song goes,
and maybe, old-timer, you can give me your
blessing, clean the dust from the needle,
and turn on the music, loud and clear,

and who cares if the upstairs neighbors complain
to the landlord and there's a knock on the door
in the middle of night but no one is home, no
one has ever been home, I can't find my way home
but I did, that was then, this is now, and here I am
watching the grass grow, watching the squirrels
climb up the trunk of a tree and down the other side
as if there was no tomorrow, no blood flowing
through the veins, no out-reach to distant stars, but
an ice cube in a glass and the dregs at the bottom
of a coffee cup will be enough for today so sleep tight
and say hello to the Big Bopper from yours truly.

INTERMEZZO

1

There are always mitigating circumstances.
Breaking and entering? Case dismissed.
Your license has been revoked.
Your whole life is under review.
The polls are in: "Some Enchanted Evening"
topped "Oh My Papa" three to one
in the red states. Age is relative—let's
enjoy ourselves while it lasts.
Some headless character actor
summons me from the wings
to play his part, but I forget the lines
and make them up as I go along. Violins,
oboes, bass fiddle, drums. Sum of parts
equals whole, whole equals nothing.
Plea-bargain, flea-ridden, thought-provoking.
Noun-verb clause. Words in Latin on a
one-way mirror. A room with a door
off a corridor, and a key.

2

He cursed at the cabdriver for splashing mud
on his uniform. I had the distinct impression that
he wasn't wearing any underwear beneath
his uniform. I wouldn't recognize you without
your uniform. A uniform is not the same as skin.
Women like men who wear uniforms.
The one-legged soldier had a crush on
the young prostitute. She would never

have noticed him without his uniform.
He folded his uniform over the back

of a chair. I was embarrassed to be
with him when he was out of uniform.

3

Anyone listening would say
you were lying through your teeth,
a little excess wedded to chance.
Forgive the dramatics,
but it could be yesterday:

you were walking down the beach
with X or riding up the coast
with Y or waking up with Z (or
no one—in H's apartment
on 5th Street—the sun
coming in.)

I want to light a candle
so we can see all her scars.
Infinity is like an arrow.
Strike my name from the list.

4

A girl in lipstick, high heels,
a demolished building north of the Grand Concourse,
a park where we might dream
of taking off our clothes,
a bed in Flushing and another in Ithaca,

End Bar (on acid),
        you got married, the day you gave birth—
    eguard chair at Far Rockaway after dark
    the movie theater in Far Rockaway where I fell
        asleep in the front row
the little Saab you drove at dawn—from 10th
        Street to Harlem—
a closet where you hid when my mother came home—
the back room at Figaro's which I passed yesterday
        and where we sat
50 years ago late afternoons—
we knew what the future held in store, but
        didn't care—
"Let's go see *Hiroshima, Mon Amour* one last time—"
Let's go to the Cloisters.
Let's end the war.

5

It's hard to think of
you in any way other than
I already do, a sequel to love
and its brief epiphany
without their love what would
we ever do? stand on a street corner
and think things over
the chastity of the blue is
in the future
"troubled fortunes and chaste lives"
I'm hiding this from you
saw you across a room but didn't speak
a woman named Trish might call
and I'd tell her you're still asleep
how to be less recondite

without disturbing
the hermit's tranquility? lead
me not into temptation etc. let's
cross the surface of the world
where the punishment of love
is its own presumption
seen from a distance between the shadings.

6

It will be I, looking out the window, and you, calling my name
     from the street.

Or it will be I, on the street, calling your name, and you, at
     the window, throwing down the key.

Or (the next day) I see you coming from a distance—an hour
     late, as usual, but with no excuses.

Waiting at the window—expectancy, anxiety, terror.

The phone was ringing—you were late—I didn't pick up. And
     then you were there, walking along the parkway, as if
     no one cared.

There were the cars going by along the parkway, and you—

It was a school day, we were staying home so we could be
     together, our only chance.

My parents were at work. It would seem like every moment
     was precious—

but there you were, walking along the parkway as if we had
all the time in the world.

And there I was—waiting for you at the window. Just like
always.

7

You can say "Satisfaction guaranteed"
and not really mean it. The difference
between what you say and what
you mean is about two feet, maybe
more. Sometimes it looks bigger when

you close your eyes. The imagination
plays tricks, always has, always will,
but just go with it for a minute, go with
me, through the door, out into the night,
up Suffolk Street, down Avenue A,
a guy in a hockey jersey smoking outside
a bar. Can I use the bathroom? It does
not seem like a difficult question.
You might give me a dirty look if you
were the bartender and I didn't buy a
drink. I just used the bathroom.
There must be something more important,
or so you would think. The philosophy
of history might be of some importance.
Aristotle, Plato, and everyone who
came before. You can think of anything,
and it might mean something, at least
for a minute, and maybe I'll have
a drink after all, if you insist.

8

Midtown traffic came to a halt
this afternoon and the shock-
waves reverberated in the suburbs,
a pot bubbling on a stove

in an empty house, rooms
crowded with combustibles
and all the litter, the love letters,
the stones picked up from a beach
with their perfect blue cuticles
of color, the mess of it all
that will remain long after
you're gone. That's how the song

goes, after you're gone I won't
forget you, the line of taxis
in the rain outside Penn
Station as I cross against the light,

*coming home, coming home, coming
home.*

NOT GUILTY

It's possible to look at things through someone else's
eyes. There are seagulls flying in a circle around the end
of the dock. I'm sitting in the aisle seat of the airplane
and the man next to me is sleeping. In Anchorage, I bought
a bottle of Johnny Walker at the duty free store and five
cartons of Marlboros. Headlights rush towards you as
you cross the parkway at midnight. You can hear what
the last dictator murmured before he died, surrounded
not by people he had loved or once loved or even distant
relatives, but only the least prominent of his lackeys,
those who were above giving love. This is the repercussion
of a feeling that won't go away. The little ash from the
tip of my cigarette drops into nowhere. Old songs on the
radio, ambulance sirens everywhere, can I please speak
to the operator? No one wants to comply with the rules
someone else has written. The leaves, by definition, are
clinging to the branches. The guy at the bus stop forced
me to fork over my bus pass. Our parents left us alone
in the forest with stars for markers. A herald arrives with
a message rolled in parchment. Can't turn your back
on what you want as if it didn't exist. Porcelain vase
(Ming Dynasty), finger in socket, last gasp.

SILENCE OF THE YAMS

I toed the line from Boca
Raton to Secaucus. My memory

bank was robbed at gunpoint
by a woman in a sari and

a man in a dress. "I confess,"
he said, "to everything," when

the police tied him to a chair.

Need some air freshener?

You can dip your
finger into the honey pot

one last time before it gets too
late, but don't be disappointed

if you come up empty. So much
for the forbidden games

that used to occupy my imagination.
Too young to know better, too old to cry.

My bonnie lies over the ocean etc.

NO TOMORROW

Sometimes it's too difficult to see in the dark. It takes about a half-hour for your eyes to adjust. The most you can ever see are outlines—the shape of a person's face, for instance, or the corner of a table.

You bump against the table and pass out on the living room rug. You fall off the ladder while hanging the curtains. It's best to consult a doctor if the wound doesn't heal. Sometimes it's best to let nature take its course, even if you wind up dead or disabled.

You can see the ocean through the tinted windows of the bus. It's a familiar story, with different characters, in a different century. Even the Puritans developed astigmatism.

The transition takes place in the middle of a sentence. It seems like you can change directions without looking back. Don't get lost in the past, you won't meet anyone you know. It isn't something I had planned to do but there it was, staring me in the face like yesterday's papers.

Weird how all your days culminate with the rays of light from tar. Once I walked out in the middle of night in a strange looking for food. I found it all right but it tasted horrible.

T
line back in time to the person I once was. The scent of the in summer, the blimp out the kitchen window. All tym you ever read and can't remember. First violinist, the girl with the harp.

SHOW OF HANDS

There's always a last time and a first time
For everything—you meet your double where
He left you on the sidewalk long ago—
There are many street corners where last
Conversations took place—a door slammed
And he walked out and she never saw him again—
The boat is turning around and coming back
To the harbor—we begin where we left off
Years ago, it's like a song—Let your mind
Go blank for a minute and her face appears—
It could be anyone, knocking at your door
For no reason

It's time to settle into my lawn chair and watch
The grass grow, if you know what I mean—a boy
On a dance floor steps on the young girl's toes—
It's like the trailer for an old movie that won't
Go away—and now he leads her back to her chair—
His hair covers his eyes and he can't see anything—
And what could he say if he could and who cares?

It's sticky fingers in this life so I better go home
Before the chair collapses under my weight
And my ship comes in one minute too late
(or too soon) and you can't give away something
You don't have to someone you don't know
(Branches of the old elm swaying in the wind,
No vanity)

NEW PANTS

I was caught with my pants up. With
my pants down. Does it matter?

I went to the dressing room and hung my
pants on a hook on the door. I mean

the pants I was wearing (and which were
wearing out) as opposed to the pants

I was trying on. Sometimes I bring more
than one pair of pants into the dressing

room. I misjudge what I look like now in
comparison with what I looked like

then, as if (in the long term, the long haul)
anyone cares. I tried on a pair

of new pants and opened the door of the
dressing room so I could see myself in

the mirror. "They look o.k.," a little voice said,
it was coming from inside my head,

as I took off the new pants and put on the old,
took the pair of new pants

to the cashier and paid for them,
more or less.

AS A TEENAGER

As a teenager
I liked to eat

off my own plate
and scrape the left-overs

into the latrine
and before you noticed

I had slipped away
even though the party

went on all night
and the last guests

stumbled out the door
and slept in the rain

with no one to blame
but myself, and a few others

and when I woke up
you were really there

like the *Odalisque*
by Manet

drinking a Bloody Mary
and braiding your hair.

ON THE WESTERN FRONT

for Katt Lissard

1

A feint to the left and he was
out in the open court, where
anything was possible, morning
till midnight, and then it was

time to stare at the moon
and stars and think of people
in the past tense only, because
that's where they are, or

were, the flowers out the bedroom
window, the key on the tray, and
that's where we want them to stay,
no questions asked.

2

An angel-food cake soaked in sherry
was offered to the friends of the
diseased, but they were already half-
way out the door

by the time I arrived in full regalia
to serenade them with a version
of Dizzy's "Salt Peanuts" and the theme
from *A Summer Place.*

Meanwhile, the ghost of Xmas past
just showed up on my doorstep. (Sorry,
I don't want any.) You can read
the small print about fringe

benefits and douse the carrots
with pesticide as the night goes
on without you like Homer in the original,
all his friends and relatives eating

couscous at the local pub. More finger
food than you can imagine under one roof,
more false starts, more late night spins
with the hood down, going nowhere fast.

What looks like a mirage on
the distant horizon, beckoning
you forward and back with the wave
of a hand, as if you were dancing

the lindy with your sister in
front of a mirror or leaping
over a turnstile to escape
from the cops.

3

Even I agree we have to improve our intelligence
capabilities. I don't mean our ability to spy on other
people or intercept phone conversations. It's one
thing to train a telescope on the windows of your
neighbors as they emerge from sleep or follow
the woman next door as she enters the corner grocery
and asks the man behind the counter for a coffee

with half & half, no sugar. You can jot down every-
thing she does in your little black book and afterwards
you can report to headquarters, like they do in the
movies. The officer in charge will compliment you for
a job well done. "We've been watching her for years,"
he says, "and now we know."

4

It's important to read *Being and Nothingness*
at least once in your life, though some
would say the same about other books as
well as the thought one might read it twice
just to make sure the message sinks in. There

is no message, except "I'm sorry, I was late.
My train stopped between stations. There was
police action, or something. I'm not sure what,
but it took awhile to restore order, and then
the train continued, as if in slow motion,
stopping at one station, followed by another,
and people I don't know got off and on,
some of them sat down, but most of them
were standing, and once a man
gave his seat to a pregnant woman
who thanked him profusely."

5

It seemed like I had passed myself
off as someone different, who had changed
over night from one person to another, but maybe

it was you who sat in the sun for too long, under
duress, your dress hanging over the arm of a chair.
There were dirty dishes in the sink

from the night before and a pink streak
of light in the sky above the river.
Maybe we'll look back years from now and blot

it all out or replay the moment in living color,
the way you reached for the phone in the middle
of night and realized it was ringing in your head

and no one was home, only a voice at the end
of the line calling your name. "Wrong number,"
you said, and hung up, without thinking twice.

6

You can stack up on crackers
for the Fourth of July. Take
your inhalers just in case. They were

shipped here from Taiwan
by a little sparrow. Ventilating
machines on wheels in the

parking garage. Minutes of life
are lost until the air gauge
system filters are restored.

Surgical intervention. A movie of animals
in a state of heat. The moment
between now and when the music

stops. Flowers on the windowsill,
flowers in the dust. A confluence of random
particles, off-shore turbulence,

and flood warnings.

7

If you don't see me when I enter the bar
It's because you've already had one too many

You must take yourself home
Under your own reconnaissance

If that's the right word
But don't touch the electric fence

It will make you sad, and with head bowed
And heavy with the weight of clouds

And tears you will measure the key to
Fit the lock and place a bag of tomatoes

And plums on the kitchen table
So everyone can partake or not

But don't put your hat
On the bed for bad luck

8

A psychopath from the Smithsonian
sank his teeth into my arm.

The tops of taxis going by in the rain.

A table for three in a restaurant
overlooking the river.

A sack of sweet potatoes on the floor
of the pantry.

Don't cash in your dividends until the market
crashes.

Buy a package of eight and get one free.

A country as big as a postage stamp
where all the meters are broken.
An all you can eat buffet,
weekdays, noon till 2.

Take the wheel for a moment.
I need a nap.

9

I played my last gig at Funky
Broadway, a bed & breakfast
that had seen better days. I drank
myself under the table and ate a
fruit cup (for breakfast) and
a sugarless scone. The Old Gray

Mare was tied to a hitching post
when a man in a Stetson

riding side saddle entered
the bar with guns blazing and

the night sky was reflected in the
bathroom mirror where a guy with

lipstick on his collar fell asleep on
the cold tiles and bit his tongue when

he came back from the dead like
a heavyweight who had fallen to his

knees in the center of the ring to
sing a rendition of "Danny Boy"

(one last time) to his admiring
fans.

10

Time is like a river, no, shit, it's like
a song.

You can give away more than you take
and sleep through the night with a heavy
heart.

It's possible you have lead poisoning,
or maybe something you ate at a chain
restaurant on a blind date when you were
a kid

brought on an attack of nerves. And you
never recovered.

A nurse came to take my blood
pressure and gave me a pill

to knock me out. Gladys Knight &
the Pips were singing "Midnight
Train to Georgia."

The conductor says "all aboard" but I'm
asleep on my feet.

Hang on tight or let go. It'll be over
in a minute.

11

I had cherry pie for
dessert, but the crust

was too moist.
A cop wrote me a ticket

for eating a fruit-
tart on the street.

The ghosts of love
summon me

to a lonely grave.
Seasons greetings

from the pest control guy
and his mother.

12

My boat washed up on an island where
there were a few palm trees and a couple
of squirrels. You can see the squirrels

running up one side of the tree
and down the other. The defining moment
of my life came and went, and no one noticed.

Will the author please stand up? The
houselights go on and the audience tosses
flowers onto the stage, but the author

has retired to the local pub for a game
of darts and a pint of Guinness.

13

Cold brisket waits for no one.
It comes with a baguette.

She leapt to her feet
as if someone had summoned her

from the dead. The feeling
is reciprocal.

I pull up my fly
in mixed company.

Full moon at noon.
Three songs for a quarter.

Put it in writing, just in case

I forget. A couple of Sprites

on tap? My name is Rene.
I'll take your order.

14

No fault of your own, you took
a step backwards into the past
and saw it differently

each time around, the cows on
the hillside swatting flies from
their behinds, the smell of mosquito

spray on someone else's skin
in the back of a car, a slave
to a system someone

else created, the flood warnings,
the icy windshield, the surfers on the
horizon, going home or staying

out too late so you can never go back
to where you came from, all the
false promises like flowers with

broken stems in the dust on
the side of the road, the theory
of cycles, the eternal recurrence,

paradise lost and found and then
lost again, all in one breath.

15

Today was less like the day
before yesterday than the night
before which started late and
went on without us over the roofs
of the houses

and the roadside stand selling
fresh eggs and lemonade also disappeared
from the field of vision
as we drove up a mountain
and then down the other side

This is where I came in and where
you got off but in a manner of
speaking we are both in sync
like the dogeared map on the floor of the ocean
like the crisp fries in a paper cup
I ate on my way home
from some public swimming hole
on the subway
as a kid

16

I should have known better than to think
she would meet me at the Café Bonaparte
in Paris where Roland Barthes used to hang
out. I sat in a corner, facing the door. Only a fool
would sit around for hours waiting for someone
to come, someone they didn't know (personally) but
someone they had seen from a distance, the flesh and blood,
the halo, the long vintage skirt purchased for half-price
in the Haight. You have to know when you're being

stupid, and I know I've made the same mistake before,
thinking something was going to happen when there
wasn't a snowball's chance in hell. You can flaunt
your theories until you're blue in the face, and everyone
within earshot is falling asleep. Class dismissed.
Those are my favorite words. I sit in the back
of the room waiting for the class to end. Then
I run into the streets, like an escaped convict,
like a doe in a poem by Wordsworth, bounding
over the hillside. I lie in the grass and see
the sunlight through the tops of the trees.
And at night I see the moon, staring back at me,
like an old friend.

HALL OF MIRRORS

Perhaps he returned home unexpectedly in the middle of the afternoon to find his wife in bed with the school crossing guard, a woman named Marge who smiled at everyone.

Maybe she had smiled once too often at this wife or possibly his wife had asked her in for an innocent cup of tea and they had ended up in bed together.

Possibly the guy with the knife on the bus was angry because of something that happened to him when he was a child.

Maybe his mother told him he looked like an idiot.

Maybe I bought him a drink and he told me his life story.

Maybe his father shouted at him because he spent his weekend afternoons reading books—*Ivanhoe, A Tale of Two Cities, Lorna Doone*—instead of playing outdoors with his friends, though he could never remember what the books were about an hour after he finished them.

It was hard to describe the feeling of pleasure he experienced when he went to the library and returned home with six books and put them up on the shelf above his bed and then the confusion after he started reading, thinking he should be doing something else.

Later in life, when he was in his early twenties, he married a woman who had lived in the apartment below the one he lived in with his parents, his childhood sweetheart, so to speak, and who later died in a train crash outside Utica, New York.

Maybe you've spent time in Union Station, the old train terminal in Utica.

Maybe you're reading this now, far from home, in a hotel room looking out over the ocean.

Maybe you're reading this on a bus heading down a gravel road in the middle of nowhere. Maybe the woman in front of you is wearing a hat with a wide brim.

SECOND CHANCE

Let me offer you a plate
of bowtie cookies but be careful
not to drop any crumbs on the
rug for fear the mice might
come out at night when we're
gone

Eat slowly and sit up straight
this time tomorrow we'll meet
again, like strangers in street
clothes, at the restaurant on
the corner

Do you want some more salsa
with your chips one might
say as a way of breaking the ice
after so many years of fighting our
way out of a paper bag

And it's only in the here and
now that we can make up
for lost time while the meter
is running and everything
is on hold

Just so we can sit across a table
and peel a grape and stare into
the space between each other's
eyes and write the definitive version
of what never happened
and never will

Drop a tincture of snake oil on
the scar tissue and pay off
your debts two at a time
while all the buildings where we spent
the night crumble into dust

And old friends greet us with
a standing ovation as I eat
the cherry at the bottom of the glass
in one bite and ask the waitress
with green eye shadow for a dry martini
straight up

THE OPEN AIR THEATER MOVES INDOORS

One time I turned the radio up loud in my head
I changed the station until someone was saying my name

There were things that needed more attention
        than others
Like people, but we shifted gears just in time

Taking Route 1 and then sleeping on the side
Of the road, the broken windshield, the flat tire,
        bugs in the engine,

The way everything goes wrong
When you first start out

"You can bet on it" they say
And then look the other way

As if one had all the time in the world to dissemble
The things that mattered most, "hailstones

The size of golfballs" the weather lady said
I'd like a tankard of porridge, if you don't mind

Next time I was singing a song in my head
It was "Strawberry Fields Forever"
        when a cloud passed in front of the sun

Everyone celebrates the first day of the new year
        in a different way
I mean every person once removed resembles
        someone else in due time

There were little things that mattered
Like a gate into the great unknown

Someone took my hand and led me out of the
        burning building
Someone left the light on in the hall—I was frightened
        (but not of the dark)

TO THE LIGHTHOUSE

My tear ducts have dried up
and I need some eyedrops. Is
the pharmacy still open? Visine,
give me some Visine please.
You can buy it over the counter.
The last thing I want is to get
dressed and go out. There's an all-
night pharmacy on Seventh
Avenue in Manhattan. I can
hear the woman behind
the counter say, "I'm sorry,
we don't have any." She likes
to work the all-night shift.
Almost no one ever comes in between
two and six and sometimes she
gets a chance to read her book,
Fear and Trembling, by Kierkegaard.
It's not bad to go to school by
day and work in the pharmacy at night.
Then she sleeps for a few hours
in the morning, if she can,
and the noise from the
nearby construction site doesn't keep
her awake. They start about eight,
the time when she gets home,
and they go nonstop till nightfall.
You can detonate a building
with a stick of dynamite
and build another. There are many
construction sites throughout the city.
The construction workers take a break
and smoke cigarettes on the street. The

woman who works in the pharmacy
pulls the sheet over her head
to drown out the sound of the
drills. They are tearing up the street
to repair a water main that exploded
during the night. The street is
closed—no traffic allowed. Sometimes
she reads in bed until her eyes grow
tired. "I'm sorry," she says, mascara
running down her cheeks, "we're out
of stock." I can see the tears in her
eyes and wonder why she's crying
real tears in front of a stranger
with dry eyes. Possibly something
in the book by Søren Kierkegaard
which she reads when there are
no customers at the all-night
pharmacy made her burst
into tears, but we'll never know.
A bell rings when I walk
through the door to announce
my arrival and the woman folds
her book face up on the counter,
Fear and Trembling, a book
I read when I was in college.
"Do you have any Visine?"
"Aisle 6," the woman behind
the counter says. There's only
one bottle of Visine on the bottom
shelf. The woman behind the counter
hands me a receipt. It's
just a matter of time before
her shift is up and she goes
home, crawls into bed with
a book, burying her head under

the pillow to block out the
noise of early morning traffic,
the drivers cursing one another
as they vie for a parking space,
and all the voices of the construction
workers shouting to each
other in languages she doesn't
understand. First, she'll go to the
bathroom in the pharmacy
and refresh her makeup. She
has rings under her eyes,
deep pockets of flesh,
from not enough sleep.
A radio is playing in the
background of her dreams,
"Clair de Lune," perhaps, by
Claude Debussy. The construction
workers say hello to her
as she walks down the street, home
from work, at eight in the morning,
some of them ogling her
as she wanders by,
and she smiles at them
as if they were old friends
whom she sees every day.
Soon the building will be finished;
rent for a 2-bedroom apartment
is $6,000 a month. The woman
who works in the pharmacy lives
in a rent-controlled apartment.
The landlord offered her a buyout,
but she turned him down. Two
drops of Visine is all I need.
I put the bottle in the medicine
cabinet next to my prescription

medicine. Don't ask me what it
is. I take Ambien every night.
They say that after a year or two
psychotic reactions set in,
but I can't fall asleep without it.
I wake up before dawn and stare
out the window where I used
to see an expanse of sky, facing
west. Now all I see is a wall
of windows and the people in
the new apartment building, getting
undressed and fucking on the
newly-washed sheets, draping
the sheets over their heads
like nuns, before turning off
the lights. There are still some
stars in the sky and an airplane
in the distance over the top
of the new building which blocks
my view, and I'd like to go
to sleep as well but it's not
that simple, even though I've
taken an Ambien (10 milligrams)
and now I'm drinking my
second cup of tea. I wish I
had some Advil PM but I don't
want to get dressed and go
down to the all-night pharmacy
to get them, but maybe I will.
The people upstairs are playing
disco music and I can hear
the beat through the floor of their apartment,
which is the ceiling of mine, and
I'm tempted to go upstairs and knock
on their door and tell them to turn

down the music, or call the police.
I've never called the police
about anything and I'm not going
to start now. "Where can I find
the Advil PM?" I ask the security
guard who works the nightshift
at the all-night pharmacy. The
woman who usually works there,
Lilla, called in sick earlier. She can't
get out of bed, or so she said, and there's a
replacement worker waiting patiently
behind the counter reading *Tender
Is the Night* by F. Scott Fitzgerald,
another book I read when I was in
college, in a class on 20th Century
American fiction, starting with
Hemingway, Fitzgerald, Willa
Cather, Gertrude Stein, Raymond
Chandler, William Faulkner, Zora
Neale Hurston, Nella Larson, Jane
Bowles, among others, some of whom
are well known, others who should
be better known, and this was just
the start. I pay for the Advil PM.
I pay the woman behind the counter,
at least a decade younger than
the woman who usually works the
night shift, who is "home with the flu,"
according to Al, the security guard,
but it was just an excuse to spend
time with her boyfriend who lives
out-of-town and was visiting her in
New York "on business" for a few
days, so at the exact moment that I
was buying Advil PM at 2 in the morning

at the pharmacy the lady who works
there, Lilla, was in bed with her boyfriend,
Henry, making love, more than once,
or so I could see from my window,
when I returned home and swallowed
two Advil PM to go along with the Ambien
which I had taken before I went
to the pharmacy, in the new high-rise
where I'm living ever since I broke up
with my wife, or she broke up with me,
even though the rent is way beyond my
means, the two bodies intertwined
on the bed, the woman on top
of the man, whose chest is almost
hairless, and then in the reverse position, with
the overhead light on and the curtains
wide open so I could see everything,
wishing I was him, and that she
was my girlfriend, the woman
who works in the pharmacy, and that
I was making love to her as I used to do
with my wife, who I first met
in Professor Abercombe's American
Literature seminar, where we sat
opposite one another around a table
with ten other students,
all of whom I remember clearly,
as I do Professor Abercombe, with
his thick black-framed glasses,
and his striped ties, which
he often removed during class,
as if he was about to take
off his clothing, starting with
his tie, then his shoes,
socks and pants, then his

underwear (boxer shorts),
and dive naked into a swimming
pool, as my wife and I
once did when we were staying
in a motel in Montauk
for the weekend, not far
from the famous lighthouse,
with the sound of the
ocean in the distance, some
fishing boats on the horizon,
and the fog coming in.

BLUE MOON

There are some buzzwords you
need to know if you want to get on
in the world, keep up with
current events, for instance, but
I don't know what they are.
Meanwhile, *The Planets* by Gustav
Holst is playing on late night
radio, coming to you from the dead
zone, this side of the Hudson.
A turn in the road and you'll find
your place, though you didn't know
you had one before this moment.
If you go too fast you might mis-
read the sign and think that
you're somewhere else, which often
happens in the course of life,
like cutting in on a couple when
they're dancing the polka,
or walking around in the rain
in Constitution Square in Athens,
the drops falling on your head
one at a time.

INTERMISSION

You can't stand around and not do anything. The ball is in
your court, and it's up to you to act appropriately, or against
the grain, with all the conviction of a person who announced
that he was going to get a drink at intermission and was
never heard from again. All you can tell the detective, a young
man with a narrow tie, and a gaunt, hungry expression,
who looked like he had wet the cuffs of his trousers stepping
absent-mindedly across a puddle, that you had last seen your
companion at intermission, or right before, when he said that
he had to go to the bathroom, urgently, and if there was time
for a glass of wine, that too was a possibility. The detective
rocked on his heels and stared furtively at my shoes, at the
space between his shoes and mine, as if the answer was
somehow hidden beneath the floorboards, as if my friend's
heart was still beating, like in the story by Poe, even though
the body had been cut into a million pieces, and the longer we
stood around the more likely I would confess to putting my
friend in harm's way, that I knew all too well at the moment
we were talking he was locked in the trunk of a used Toyota
hurtling up the Taconic Parkway, surrounded by a blaze
of fall foliage, and that it was only a matter of time before
the highway patrol discovered him kneeling naked on the
shoulder of the road, bleeding from a wound in his forehead.
The story continued but by then the show was over and the
crowds mingled in the lobby, opening their umbrellas against
the downpour, and stepping out into the rain to hail a taxi,
the chill wind blowing through their bones. All the spoiled
makeup and haughty coiffures of yesterday meant nothing in
the face of the storm, and the long walk home down streets
paved and narrow, where no one was waiting up for me with
a glass of warm milk, and the radio was playing an old Benny
Goodman number. I forget the name.

NOBLESSE OBLIGE

Pay attention to all the details
of writing. Sentence structure, for
instance, and the use of commas.
The abyss needs some attention as
well as the void, but words
are not interchangeable, and
cellphone use is not permitted
during class. The highest grade
you can get is a D, but don't despair,
many people did poorly in school
and went on to high-paying jobs.
It's not that interesting to contemplate
the afterlife, but might be something
you do in your spare time, just for fun.
"By the Time I Get to Phoenix" was
a favorite song, but don't look back
at the high and low ends of the spectrum,
starting in the stone age with the invention
of fire, and ending in the present with the
sun disappearing behind the clouds,
and you in my arms (or not). The
moment exhausts itself like a runaway
train, the rush hour traffic on the Long
Island Expressway, the crosstown
bus no longer in service. It's not a bad
idea to walk a mile or two every day.
Let's meet for a double espresso
and a plate of humus and cheese
some late afternoon when all the kids
are in school. I had a brush with the law
when I was sixteen, I must admit, but
I dodged a bullet and they let me go free.
"If it happens again," someone said, "you'll

be in deep shit," and since that day I've
kept my nose clean, my eyes on
the message board so I know what's
coming next. I've had enough surprises
in one lifetime, to say the least. A
priest in street clothes gave us his
blessings when we picked him up on the
side of the road. "Where's the nearest Justice
of the Peace," we asked, the way city
slickers ask country folk if they can milk
a cow, and the man in the back seat
answered, "You've come to the right
place, I'm him."

IN SPITE OF EVERYTHING

for Rackstraw Downes

The emergency medical worker
Stretching his legs in the parking
Lot of the local hospital,

The tour guide taking a piss
In the bathroom of Shaker Village,
The half-naked woman leaning

Out the tenement window
Calling the man in shorts
Home for dinner, the air

Train delay from Newark Airport
To Penn Station and the man on the
Intercom announcing that full

Service has been restored, the left-
Over sushi, the woman
Sitting on the side of the bed

Watching cable news, a slice of
Stale toast with jam, the wall
Covered with graffiti, the bags

Of garbage in the deserted lot, the
Mountain climber's fall, the cemetery
Plot, the words on the gravestones,

The Abbott at the door of the
Monastery, the bark of a tree
When you're hungry,

The book on your knees
When you're falling asleep,
The dud avocado, the overdue mortgage,

The bare-chested men on the street corner
Playing dominos, a turkey and her brood
Crossing the road.

STEVE'S

No one asked but
I know a modestly priced
Barber named Steve

He has a barbershop
On the main street of town

His partner is also named Steve
Which is why the shop
Is called "Steve's"

Mostly, the younger Steve cuts my hair
And clips my eyebrows
And shaves my sideburns

If it's too crowded
You can always go to Moe's
Just down the street

People rave about Moe's
But I've never been
I go to Steve's and read the newspaper

And wait my turn,
And then, a few
Months later, I return

With a lot more hair

SILENT MOVIE

I disappeared through
the eye of a pin and came
out the other side. You will
regret everything you ever
said about anyone.

You can pretend you don't
remember who kissed who,
or what happened the night of June 3rd,
1960, when you went on a blind
date and never returned.

You can buy some comic relief
over the counter, a small dose
before you go to sleep, one pill with
every meal. Some Belgian waffles
with a side order of grits

might hit the spot around now.
The sidewalks are filled with people
who like to smoke, but don't.
Instead, they shuffle by in their boots.
Some soporific platitudes might

be in order, an alphabet of long silences
and shortness of breath. We can
forego the antipasto and start with
the dessert. For once in our lives,
nothing matters but the footnotes
at the bottom of the page. I need a seat
on the aisle so I can make my escape.
Sometimes I have to go to the bathroom

before the first act is over. Sometimes
there's only one act, and the stage is empty.

RAPID RESPONSE

I slipped away at the first light
Of dawn and slept on the ground, a stone
For a pillow. It's possible to travel
(In your head) from the Belle Epoque to the present
Some things are different, but many things are the same
And there's more than enough to keep you busy during
     the day
And far into the night
I slipped away when no one was looking
And stared at myself in the bathroom mirror
I was a child thinking of death for the first time
My body against the sink to make sure I was still
     alive
And this was what I felt
The cold sink against my skin—it was one way of thinking
You could touch someone in the dark and that was enough
"Living" and "touching" were almost the same
Part two was to remember what it felt like afterwards
Sometimes it happens outdoors, on an empty beach
A chill in the air when you step out of the water
Your mother wraps a towel around your naked shoulders
Sometimes it happens in sleep when you fall through a hole
     in the sky
And land on the other side
Or step off a train that's still moving
Once I stared into space and couldn't come back
From where I had gone and where I had been
And the hands of the clock moved forward but I couldn't breathe
A boat adrift on the ocean with no land in sight
I can change into another person if you want
It's enough to see the light come up over the tops of the hills
And the clouds in the distance, the blocks

Of ice cracking like a broken heart, a radio
On the beach in La Paz playing our song.

ONE DRINK MINIMUM

Backwards, up or down,
straight forward: these

are the ways to go. Don't
cash in your dividends

before the market crashes.
Toss your laundry into the

hamper and carry it down
the hall. I'm not talking

about myself necessarily
but someone I used to know.

Maybe it was a car door
that slammed in the night?

It's not a good idea to back
yourself into a corner

office without so much as
a window facing the murky

waters of the Gowanus. The
night is young, but the slumber

party is almost over. I'm
just writing to let you know

your subscription has perspired.

DON'T TELL ANYONE

& so I let go of you for a moment
in the triangle of thoughts
in which one idea bleeds into
another and another replaces
the one that was left behind
the one who couldn't find
his place, unlaced his sneakers,
and fell asleep
since the end of the race
is where those who have lost
wreak havoc on the few
who are still left standing

I let go, before the end,
it was like walking across a bridge
with the traffic below us
in the late afternoon rush
and in the distance there were flowers
and townhouses and a bride and groom
on the steps of a church

There was the church. It looked old
like a hand-me-down sweater
with marks of desire in every vestibule
and someone's god depicted
in stained glass in every window
the groom already half asleep
pockmarked skin already dissolute
like an adolescent boy
carving his initials in a tree
the boy was not me but the shadows
of the spire were already extending

outward over the fallen leaves
and I wanted to protect someone
as if it was part of a plan

So I let go of you for a moment
there was the bridge and the particles
of sand on the windswept beach
and the trolley tracks leading nowhere
and a fissure in space where everything
disappeared when you weren't looking
all of marriage & love
in the same ball of complicity
tied up forever
like a ball of fire
over the sea

All of it coming to me like a period
at the end of a sentence & when you erased
the period the words continued
like guns and flowers, like madmen with sticks
to divine some wisdom where before there
were only skid marks
and some bleak testimony
which you couldn't even give away
at the end of the street

It could be that you backslide
maybe once in a blue moon
and remember the time you scalded
your hand on the rusty kettle
a nurse was called in in the middle of
night to wrap a sodden tourniquet around your wound
it isn't worth talking about, but it would make you
blink to think of the past as a promontory
where you can step over the edge

whenever you want
and discover
someone you know

Look through the keyhole and see who's there
in restaurants and bars, the people smoking on street corners
the wherewithal to remove the tenant
from the apartment by throwing his possessions
out the window. "We're happy to have you on board,"
or so they say. But wait until they learn
my true colors

WEAK IN THE KNEES

No one has said otherwise
so please continue

you can leave the way you came
and no one will care

in warm weather you can wear a slip
with flowers on the hem

I can sit around and throw
a tantrum to get your attention

It's not a matter of what
anyone says, or when,

or the mastery of words
in a mother tongue

look it up in the dictionary
if you want to know what it means

or cast a spell
on the army of shadows

it's not like someone is
dictating the words from above

they all come out at the
same time every night

I am in the forest and you
are in the clouds

someone you don't know
is breathing at the other end

you think you are on the right
path you can change in a minute

I was sitting in the corner and you
came over and told me your name

you might as well sink under
the sheets and call it a day

or visit a Gothic Cathedral
with a friend of a friend

you can call me any time
917 856-2747

but don't take it personally
if I don't answer

I am obviously not myself
and you are only you

if we make too much noise
the neighbors will complain

Something you did
in the past may come back

to haunt you in another life
I want to change my name

move to a different city
and start all over

with a new hairdo

NOT FAR

It was 1940-something, believe it
or not, and I was wearing a bib. I probably
spilled some food on my shirt, as
I sometimes still do. The laundry piles
up almost over night, so you have to be
careful what you wear. I tend to get
glue all over everything, if you want the truth.
My pants are covered with glue. You
can't wash it out. You can't make this stuff
up. There's a laundromat down the street.
I need four quarters to use the machine.
All you have to do is ask and I'll give
you change. It's not that simple. I scooped
up the food on the tip of my fork
and it landed on my shirt. My mother
tied the bib around my neck. It didn't
hurt. I had learned my lesson, if there
was one to learn. You can learn something
new every day, if you try. If you read
the same book more than once it begins
to sink in. Sometimes I read more
than one book at a time. My right eye
is better than my left. It sees things
differently, but sometimes the words begin
to blur. My eyes get tired when I stay
up late. I used to be able to stay up all
night in the nineteen sixties. I liked to
look out the window at the first light
of morning on St. Mark's Place. Once
I saw W.H. Auden walk by carrying
The London Times. He lived down
the street. Here's a picture of me eating

breakfast when I was a kid. There's
a blimp out the window frozen in the
sky above the Bronx and the radio
is playing "I'm Walking Behind You"
by Eddie Fisher. "I'm walking behind
you," he's singing, sadly "on your wedding
day." That's my mother in the background
with a bib, just in case I spill something
on my shirt. It's the first day of school.
I can't walk out the door with a stain
on my shirt. They will think my mother
is neglecting me. They'll send a social
worker to the house. How can you send
your child to school with jam on his
shirt? That didn't happen, until my own
daughter went to school. The teacher
sent her home at lunch because she had
a stain on her blouse, and a social
worker called up, and I shouted at him
(I must admit) over the phone. It was
1982 and the snow was falling on the
streets of the Lower East Side, where
my parents were born and where I was
living now. My parents couldn't believe
it when they visited me in my apartment
not far from where they lived when
they were children. My mother's mother
had a heart attack on the subway and died.
She rested her head on the shoulder
of a stranger and closed her eyes. The
apple does not fall far from the tree. Or
something. Men with chainsaws arrive
to cut down the tree, and I'm driving
down a road in the country, going
nowhere fast, not far from where

Leonard Bernstein conducted the Boston
Symphony at Tanglewood when he was
twenty-five, not far from where Serge
Koussivitsky is buried in the Lenox Cemetery.
You can start off somewhere and go
somewhere else, in your thoughts, at any
rate, which are your own and no one
else's, and no one knows, for a second,
what's going on inside anyone, all the
people you see in the subway or pass
on the street, the people in the cars
who honk their horns because you're going
too slow, who pass you on the right,
who look at you as if you are some old
gray-haired dude who's lost his way, or
who had too much to drink at dinner,
a Manhattan with a cherry, and maybe
another, but be careful not to spill any
down the front of your shirt, and good luck
to you all on the long drive home.

SOMEONE I KNOW

It was fun to watch the man in the pizzeria toss
the dough into the air. I pressed my nose
against the glass, wanting more than I could give.

I practiced my swing in the mirror
when everyone was asleep
and rolled up the cuffs of my trousers

as I jumped over the puddles.
I unlocked the door of someone else's house
and wiped my shoes

on the welcome mat. It was a home
away from home, and I never went back.
You must let the other come in, and see what

happens, even if it means standing on a subway
platform like a statue in the cold. Even if it means
waiting up all night just to hear her key in the door.

It's a different soundtrack for the same movie I
watched long ago, where everyone looks cross-eyed
as they stare into the sun, a cash only, no money

down, 3-month guarantee type of nothingness,
something we can skim over (if we want)
in our spare time, when we're traveling

like ghosts from one city to another,
and even the dining room is closed, the quiet
car is empty, and the only people

in the station are the members
of the local high school hockey team
with their sticks in the air

waiting for a van to take them
to a game with their main rivals
one town over.

I'm putting it all on the back burner
for awhile, where everything happens,
where we all live and die,

a shopping cart filled with boxes
of detergent to wash out the stain,
but don't forget to turn off the gas and lock

the gates on the windows
before you go outside.
The Queen of Hearts

is waiting for you in a marked car,
with her foot on the brake, so fasten your
seatbelt one last time,

and hold tight.

SINGLE OCCUPANCY

for Archie Rand

All of your mornings begin in the same way

There are many things to do—at any given moment there are
    many things to do—and it's important not to forget
    any of them

Nothing stands between the precipice and the ledge

A tornado watch is in effect until midnight, and all the midnights
    to come

Give credit where it's due, or claim it as your own

It's a good idea to go AWOL and spend the night on dry land

The children on the beach chasing a ball into the tide

Equate "maturity" with the ability to take care of yourself, but
    something goes wrong

They came out of nowhere and disappeared into the night

This is the room where I lost my virginity

Children appear out of nowhere to eat the leftovers

The midnight train to Georgia is leaving in a few minutes

Rapunzel let down her hair and rode out of town

Look at me for a moment when you have a moment

You were playing in the streets with your friends
    and it was time for dinner

The stun-gun comes in handy when an unexpected visitor
    appears at your bedroom door

Crawl back into your cave until the storm subsides

Two for the price of one, a half-dozen of the other

No one told you what it was like to run naked through the grass

This office is closed until further notice

There's a diner around the bend where you can get coffee
    to go and a slice of pie

This is the road where we got lost in the fog

A can of paint thinner was left out in the rain

I missed the turn-off and landed in the swamp

Nothing can prevent me from having my own thoughts

A kid in short pants with a chip on his shoulder

A cop in uniform shopping for sheets at Target

Why not give yourself the present you think you deserve?

I forgot what I wanted to tell you, put the check in the mail

A line outside the porta-potty from dusk till dawn

Stop me if I'm confusing you with someone else

Keep your mouth shut and nothing will happen to you
    or your friends

The riders on the storm are waiting for you around the bend

The names of all the stars and planets are on the tip of my
    tongue

No one knows about any of this except me

Remember to close the windows when you leave the house

She lived on the same street all her life, I kid you not

Write down the words you won't get a second chance

I went in one door and came out the other

Surprise me for once in your life and arrive on time

All I can offer you is some warm papaya juice, and a spittoon

It's possible to fall in love with everyone you meet,
    at least for a minute

The concourse of reckless abandon is open to everyone

Slip into something cool and join me on the patio

You are barred from these premises until further notice

The last time I drove through town I had a tuna melt
    and a Coke

Here I am, in broad daylight, the person I once knew

He was a stranger in his own country who was talking
    off the top of his head

You can drop me at the corner of Forgive & Forget

Here, in the dark, it doesn't matter what you're wearing

How about a night on the town at your favorite bistro?

You can always get a raincheck and come back tomorrow

It was right in front of my nose but I didn't see it

The wedding will go on, whether you're there or not

Come back to where you were, never leaving, never
    saying goodbye

The apartment comes with a hot plate and a tub

How many times can you say "goodbye" in one day?

The great neon bulb went out above my head

The wolf at the door begins to bark when I say your name

I pause under the streetlight and stare at her window

It's all happening off-stage, whether you like it or not

I bagged some groceries at the checkout counter of the empty
    heart and ate a corn muffin in the pouring rain

"The drinks are on me," one might say, and leave it at that

You can lie to yourself, ad infinitum, even as you sleep

You had offered me something—your hand?—and now you were
taking it away

A date in the future when you must vacate the premises

Someone I didn't know was standing under the shower

If you listen to the music you might dissolve the tension—two
left feet, quicksand and chaos

The person I was kissing had changed her name

We snacked on sugarless gum and ate day-old donuts, three
for a quarter

A split personality sleeping on the couch of a friend

You can roll back the tide and see what's coming, even before
it happens

Offer something for half-price no one wants

A loop of the same song reverberating in your head

An object enters your line of vision and you give it a name

I'm free seven days a week, afternoons and evenings

A tornado watch is in effect until midnight

Dissolve two aspirin in a spoon and swallow

Brief flashes of happiness, colorless hair

We hold our breath in the back of the cab and close
      our eyes

Portents of the future, harbingers of the past

(It was all in your mind from start to finish)

It would seem like love could last a long time if you let it

You can spread your blanket on the sand and toss
      a beach ball into the air

Audrey Hepburn crawls across the kitchen floor
      with a knife in her teeth

I beg the reader to forgive me in advance

It's pointless to get down on your knees and weep
      for no good reason

The judge tacked a day onto your sentence, which ends here

You have to wait in line for a drink at intermission

If you go to the well once too often, you fall in

The planes are stranded on the runway and the ice is melting
      on the wing

The phrase "no stone unturned" does not apply

I wiped my boots on the welcome mat and begged for more

You can park in front of a hydrant and no one will write you
    a ticket

The worms are squirming at the bottom of the can

I was playing blind man's bluff in a room of my own

A man stands on a table and takes off his pants

The hours in between feel like nothing at all, like years

The volunteer rubble runs into the fireman

You have one thing on your mind, and it's better than nothing

Dispense with your outer garments and cross against the green

It was like yesterday, today and tomorrow rolled into one

What you know now through memory who you are
    adds up to nothing

It takes a while for the truth to sink in

Pigments of desire among the glossy shadows

NIGHT INSECTS IN THE TREES

1

The crime scene was cordoned off
so no one could tinker with
the evidence

except me. Who's in charge here,
anyway? Dead or alive,
what matters most

is that you left your signature
on the bottom line and crossed
against the green into the oncoming
traffic and bit your lip when the cargo

plane landed on the water and the pilot
and all the passengers
were rescued by a passing barge.

It's time to lay low for awhile,
and assume different
identities,

dance the cha-cha
in front of a live audience,
step off the curb
into the abyss.

There's something happening
elsewhere, but it's just
out of reach. "Beyond my grasp"
you might say, and take your bows.

2

You can swallow the pill
or dissolve it in water. A new
weather system every minute:
true or false?

An innocent bystander,
not true. A mango smoothie,
not applicable. A white naugahyde
couch. Possession with intent.

A roll of duct tape. The
prosecution rests its case.
A piebald terrier. Court
adjourned.

False eyelashes, cut flowers.
Go take a hike. A 20 minute
delay at the entrance to the
Holland Tunnel?

See you shortly.

3

Soon I'm the only one still sitting in the cheap seats.
Maybe if you're quiet you can hear the insects
in the trees. Don't concede any points to your
opponent. Don't assume the people who look you
in the eye are telling the truth.

An X-ray machine, a leaky pen.
Internal patterns of branches and leaves.
The story of the pestilence and the seven plagues.

The words of warning on the side of a can.
Inexplicable, this burned out forest
on the side of the road. The words pass through
one ear and linger in the other.
They seem to stick around until it's all a blank.

Her mouth is moving but the words are cast adrift
like snowflakes on the windshield you have to
wipe them off by hand.

4

Some images act
as an aid to memory: a man
with one ear,
a 3-legged dog

limping down the street.
When you begin to forget

me think about that
dog, and the empty street
at dawn with the lights
coming on in all the windows
where people no longer
in love

are waking up on either side
of their beds, backs turned
to one another, silently
buttoning their blouses
and shirts. Possibly

associating me with the man

with one ear is the preferred
mnemonic to bring me back
to you,

a kind of inner stenography,

as if instead of trying to see me
you imagined the 1-eared man
or the 3-legged dog,

and then I would appear,
in outline, like a speck on
the horizon, waving
goodbye.

5

The list of do's and don'ts never adds up.
You make a choice and pull the lever.

It's hard to sit all day in an outdoor cafe,
lingering over a coffee, when you could

be doing something no one else has done.
It's hard to know what that might be

until you're doing it. The frame of reference
changes, year to year, season to season—

"an egg stain on the sleeve of her shirt"—"a
water beetle in the sink"—"a pink streak

of light in the sky above the river."
You can leave your footprints

on the rim of the crater, turn a blind eye
to what came before. Transparent skies,

a tongue-kiss in the rain. Iron Age corpses
preserved in peat bog. Shag carpeting.

6

Out of the starting gate
onto the track.

(Once you cross the river
you can never return.)

A watered-down version
of a tree, a flower.

Black box on ocean bottom.
Dead suffragettes.

Rewind the tape
and lower the shade.

Make up for lost time
in another life.

Drown your sorrows
over a pint of malt ale.

Twist and shout to your
heart's content.

LIFE OF THE PARTY

You can focus on one thing
and see it from a distance

as if it was close up and no one
was looking, no one

was writing down your phone
number on the side of an

envelope, no one traveling
at the velocity of light, the speed

of light the distance between
one planet (mine) and yours,

you might call yourself a body
of water coming to rest

between two mountains,
from a distance you can see the

snowcapped peaks of the mountains
but when you get up close

you can see the water, the lake,
you can travel around the lake at

the speed of light, coming to you
from a planet, yours or mine,

like a cloud above the ocean
passing between you and the sun

in slow motion, it seems like
we're lying on top of the clouds,

you can stare at your reflection
on the surface of the lake, but don't

fall in, the clouds are passing I find
your number on the side of an envelope,

maybe I wrote it, or you did,
it's the wrong number, I'll call you

tonight, it seems like we're lying
down on the surface of the body of

water between two hills
on another planet, and no one cares

if we come or go, if we leave for
a short period of time and return,

if we walk down the road or come back
at our own speed, with the hills in the

distance and the sound of a train
whistle, everything happening in its

own time, if only for a moment, that's
how long anything lasts, a moment

that might be an hour or a day, it seemed
like no time had passed at all,

and there you were, as beautiful
as ever

ELIXIR

What matters most my friends are gone

See their faces, hear them speak

"I have so many regrets," he said

Ice cream, he wanted ice cream

The nurse brings me a cup of cold orange sherbet

The first thing I've eaten in days

Shklovsky's *Third Factory* and Alice's *For the Ride*

On my bedside table

I woke up thinking I was in my own bed

Shelley, the night nurse, brings me a pitcher of ice water

Everyone has a pathology—I was angry for a long time

And I didn't know why

In the middle of a fight

She put her hand through a French window

We had to take a taxi to the ER at St. Vincent's

It takes years to figure out who you are

When the surgery is over you open your eyes

You must sign a consent form, you must sign your life away

Soon I will leave the hospital and walk down the street
    like any stranger

Once I arrived without asking at her house in the middle of night
    and she let me in

There's no one around to witness these moments

There's no one here except Shelley the night nurse

The last time I was in the hospital my roommate was Lee Konitz

He died soon after—I read it in the newspaper

I listened to him sing to himself in his sleep

My roommate was discharged earlier in the day, so I'm alone

Visiting hours 3-7, we'll talk on the phone

I see all the faces of my friends every day

I met Larry Fagin in the back of Gino & Carlo, a bar in San
    Francisco, 1963

I played chess and drank beer with Lee Harwood in my apartment   .
    in Cambridge

"You can go home on Friday," the doctor says, "no reason to stay
    here any longer"

He called Katt after the surgery to assure her everything went
    well

Bill Corbett was the best man at my wedding in the country, 1975

You can begin a sentence with a capital letter and end with a
    period, or not

Bill Berkson and I embraced one last time outside EJ's, May 2016

I told Ted Greenwald I would "See him soon" and he said "You
    better come back tomorrow"

The last time I saw Joanne Kyger was after her reading at DIA,
    "Oh Lewis!"

I ate lunch with Bill Kushner at Le Grainne and I knew
    something was wrong

I'm writing from Lenox Hill, my bed near the window

Soon the light will come up over the city

The night nurse, Shelley, will bring me a Percocet, maybe two

And no doubt Dr. Newman and his team will visit and
    the day nurses will arrive

"Think of the most beautiful place," the anesthesiologist says as
    he puts me under

And my mind goes blank

Katt's face as I step from the shower and she dries my back
   and shoulders

My scrawny shoulders

Thursday 4 A.M.
June 11, 2020

FIRST COMMUNION

It was the kind of day
you could stand
under the mistletoe
and kiss anyone
who walked by
and no one cared

if it was sunny or bright
or whether time was on your side
or you were older than Methuselah

no one minded if your arm was in a sling
or your shirt was threadbare
and your laces untied
no one cried herself to sleep
or sat in the corner
while the band played on

and no one left a baby
on your doorstep
in the middle of night
or took a swan dive
into a pond
and touched bottom

no one minded if you danced
the foxtrot
with a stranger
or threw out your back
changing a tire
in the south of France

no one cared if you
stood on a street corner
hailing a cab on a hot day
or sat at the end of the bar
and ordered a coffee
with rum

or set fire to the garage
or put your hand through
a pane of glass
no one minded
if you unbuttoned your shirt
down to your waist

no one cared if you
powdered your face
or touched your toes
with your hands
no one wondered if you
were going or staying

if your train was late
or on time
no one said
"a friend in need
is a friend indeed"
without biting her tongue

No one lied on the stand
or ate carrot
cake for dessert
or called for back-up
when things got rough

No one wondered if your
heart had changed over night
if you drank too much
wine and cursed your fate

if the fountain of youth
was closed for repair
if you took the long way home
without thinking twice.

ACKNOWLEDGMENTS

Thanks to Joey Infante and Micah Savaglio, editors of Overpass Books, for publishing the poem "On the Western Front" in a limited edition chapbook (2019).

Thanks to the editors who first published these poems in their magazines and anthologies.

Special thanks to Max Warsh, Sophia Warsh, Marie Warsh, Alyssa Gorelick, Jenny and Erle Radel, Jamey Jones, Matvei Yankelevich, Susan Lewis, Charles North, Richard Roundy, John Olson, and Kyle Schlesinger.

*

Some of these poems first appeared in the following magazines and websites: *Across the Margin, Alligatorzine, Downtown Brooklyn, Hurricane Review, Lethe Literary and Art Journal, Live Mag, Mimeo Mimeo, The Poetry Project, Posit: A Journal of Art and Literature,* and *West Florida Literary Federation.*

*

The Estate of Lewis Warsh is grateful to Anna Moschovakis and Daniel Owen of Ugly Duckling Presse for all their work on *Elixir.* Some of the poems from this collection appeared in tributes to Lewis in the March 2021 issues of *The Brooklyn Rail* and *Boog City.* We thank editors Anselm Berrigan, David Kirschenbaum, and John Mulrooney for assembling those tributes.

ALSO BY LEWIS WARSH

POETRY
The Suicide Rates
Highjacking
Moving Through Air
Chicago, with Tom Clark
Dreaming As One
Long Distance
Immediate Surrounding
Today
Blue Heaven
Hives
Methods of Birth Control
The Corset
Information from the Surface of Venus
Avenue of Escape
Private Agenda, with Pamela Lawton
The Origin of the World
Debtor's Prison, with Julie Harrison
Reported Missing
Flight Test
The Flea Market in Kiel
Inseparable: Poems 1995-2005
Alien Abduction
Out of the Question: Selected Poems 1963-2003

FICTION
Agnes & Sally
A Free Man
Money Under the Table
Ted's Favorite Skirt
A Place in the Sun
One Foot Out the Door: Collected Stories

AUTOBIOGRAPHY
Part of My History
The Maharajah's Son
Bustin's Island, 1968
Piece of Cake, with Bernadette Mayer

EDITOR
The Angel Hair Anthology, with Anne Waldman

RECORDING
The Origin of the World

TRANSLATION
Night of Loveless Nights by Robert Desnos

photograph by Max Warsh

Lewis Warsh (1944-2020) was a writer, editor, visual artist, educator and the author of over thirty volumes of poetry, fiction, and autobiography, including *The Origin of the World* (2001), *Inseparable: Poems 1995-2005* (2008), *A Place in the Sun* (2010), *One Foot Out the Door: Collected Stories* (2014), *Alien Abduction* (2015), *Out of the Question: Selected Poems 1963-2003* (2017), and *Piece of Cake* (2020). He was co-founder, with Bernadette Mayer, of United Artists Magazine and Books, and co-founder and editor, with Anne Waldman, of Angel Hair Books and Magazine and *The Angel Hair Anthology* (2001). *Mimeo Mimeo #7* (2012) was devoted to his poetry, fiction and collages, and to a bibliography of his work as a publisher and editor. He was a recipient of grants from The National Endowment for the Arts, The American Poetry Review, and The Poetry Foundation. He taught at Naropa University, The Poetry Project, Pace University, The New School, Bowery Poetry Club, and SUNY Albany. A longtime member of the English Department faculty at Long Island University (Brooklyn), he was also the founding director of their MFA Program in Creative Writing (2007-13). A full bibliography and selected artworks are viewable at lewiswarsh.com.